STEP-BY-STEP

Indian Vegetarian Cooking

STEP-BY-STEP

Indian Vegetarian Cooking

LOUISE STEELE

SHOOTING STAR PRESS

This edition printed in 1995 for:
Shooting Star Press Inc
230 Fifth Avenue – Suite 1212
New York, NY 10001

Shooting Star Press books are available at special discounts for bulk purchases for sales promotions, premiums, fund-raising, or educational use. Special edition or book excerpts can also be created to specification. For details contact: Special Sales Director, Shooting Star Press Inc., 230 Fifth Avenue, Suite 1212, New York, NY 10001

ISBN 1 56924 191 0

Printed in Italy

Acknowledgements:

Design & DTP: Pedro & Frances Prá-Lopez / Kingfisher Design
Art Direction: Clive Hayball
Managing Editor: Alexa Stace
Special Photography: Martin Brigdale
Home Economist: Jill Eggleton
Step-by-Step Photography: Karl Adamson
Step-by-Step Home Economist: Joanna Craig
Stylist: Helen Trent

Photographs on pages 6, 28, 46 & 64: By courtesy of ZEFA

Contents

CHAPTER ONE

Soups & Appetizers

If a dessert is the crowning grand finale to a meal then an appetizer must be the opening overture, and should be orchestrated to tease the tastebuds and tempt the appetite. The repertoire of vegetarian Indian dishes to fulfil this role is fortunately wide and varied. Soups are a natural choice for the prepare-ahead cook and can be made thick and hearty with legumes like beans and lentils to satisfy large appetites. Some soups, like Indian Bean Soup and Spicy Dal and Carrot Soup will also double up beautifully as light lunch dishes. Others provide a lighter, more refreshing start, as in Minted Pea and Yogurt Soup.

In India, appetizers are rarely served as such, and would instead accompany a meal. These typical dishes do, however, fill the role of appetizers and are just perfect to serve with drinks at informal buffet parties. Vegetable and Nut Samosas and Garlicky Mushroom Pakoras can be made well ahead and reheated before serving, and Spiced Corn and Nut Mix makes a superb alternative to the predictable peanut and crisp offerings with drinks.

Opposite: *Transporting supplies by canoe in Kerala.*

INDIAN BEAN SOUP

A thick and hearty soup, nourishing and substantial enough to serve as a main meal with whole-wheat bread. Black-eye peas are used here, but red kidney beans or chick-peas may be added to the mixture if preferred.

STEP 1

STEP 2

STEP 3

STEP 4

SERVES 4-6

4 tbsp ghee or vegetable oil
2 onions, peeled and chopped
1½ cups potato, peeled and cut into chunks
1½ cups parsnip, peeled and cut into chunks
1½ cups turnip or rutabaga, peeled and cut into chunks
2 celery stalks, trimmed and sliced
2 zucchini, trimmed and sliced
1 green bell pepper, seeded and cut into ½-in pieces
2 garlic cloves, peeled and crushed
2 tsp ground coriander
1 tbsp paprika
1 tbsp mild curry paste
5 cups vegetable stock
salt
1 x 15-oz can black-eye peas, drained and rinsed
chopped fresh cilantro, to garnish (optional)

1 Heat the ghee or oil in a saucepan, add all the prepared vegetables, except the zucchini and green bell pepper, and cook over a moderate heat for 5 minutes, stirring frequently. Add the garlic, cilantro, paprika and curry paste and cook for 1 minute, stirring.

2 Stir in the stock and season with salt to taste. Bring to a boil, cover and simmer gently for 25 minutes, stirring occasionally.

3 Stir in the peas, sliced zucchini and green bell pepper, cover and continue cooking for a further 15 minutes or until all the vegetables are tender.

4 Purée 1¼ cups of the soup mixture (about 2 ladlefuls) in a food processor or blender. Return the puréed mixture to the soup in the pot and reheat until piping hot. Sprinkle with chopped cilantro, if using and serve hot.

COOK'S TIP

For a thinner, broth-type consistency to the soup, do not purée the 2 ladlefuls of mixture as instructed at step 4. The flavor of this soup improves if made the day before it is required, as this allows time for all the flavors to blend and develop.

MINTED PEA & YOGURT SOUP

*A deliciously refreshing soup that is full of goodness. It is also extremely
tasty served chilled – in which case, you may like to thin the
consistency a little more with extra stock, yogurt or milk.*

STEP 1

SERVES 6

2 tbsp ghee or vegetable oil
2 onions, peeled and coarsely chopped
1½ cups potato, peeled and coarsely chopped
2 garlic cloves, peeled
1-in piece gingerroot, peeled and chopped
1 tsp ground cilantro
1 tsp ground cumin
1 tbsp all-purpose flour
3½ cups vegetable stock
3 cups frozen peas
2-3 tbsp chopped fresh mint, to taste
salt and freshly ground black pepper
⅔ cup plain yogurt
½ tsp cornstarch
1¼ cups milk
a little extra yogurt, for serving (optional)
mint sprigs, to garnish

gently for 15 minutes or until the
vegetables are tender.

3 Purée the soup, in batches, in a
blender or food processor. Return
the mixture to the pot and season with
salt and pepper to taste. Blend the yogurt
with the cornstarch and stir into the
soup.

4 Add the milk and bring almost to a
boil, stirring all the time. Cook very
gently for 2 minutes. Serve hot, sprinkled
with the remaining mint and a swirl of
extra yogurt, if wished.

STEP 2

STEP 3a

1 Heat the ghee or oil in a saucepan,
add the onions and potato and
cook gently for 3 minutes. Stir in the
garlic, ginger, cilantro, cumin and flour
and cook for 1 minute, stirring.

2 Add the stock, peas and half the
mint and bring to a boil, stirring.
Reduce the heat, cover and simmer

COOK'S TIP

The yogurt is mixed with a little
cornstarch before being added to the hot
soup – this helps to stabilize the yogurt
and prevents it from separating when
heated.

STEP 3b

STEP 1

STEP 2

STEP 3

STEP 4

SPICY DAL & CARROT SOUP

This delicious, warming and nutritious soup uses split red lentils and carrots as the two main ingredients, and includes a selection of spices to give it a "kick". It is simple to make and extremely good to eat.

SERVES 6

²/₃ cup split red lentils
5 cups vegetable stock
2 cups carrots, peeled and sliced
2 onions, peeled and chopped
1 cup canned chopped tomatoes
2 garlic cloves, peeled and chopped
2 tbsp vegetable ghee or oil
1 tsp ground cumin
1 tsp ground cilantro
1 fresh green chili, seeded and chopped, or
    use 1 tsp minced chili (from a jar)
½ tsp ground turmeric
1 tbsp lemon juice
salt
1¼ cups milk
2 tbsp chopped fresh cilantro
yogurt, to serve

1 Place the lentils in a strainer and wash well under cold running water. Drain and place in a large saucepan with 3½ cups of the stock, the carrots, onions, tomatoes and garlic. Bring the mixture to a boil, reduce the heat, cover and simmer for 30 minutes or until the vegetables and lentils are tender.

2 Meanwhile, heat the ghee or oil in a small saucepan. Add the cumin, cilantro, chili and turmeric and fry gently for 1 minute. Remove from the heat and stir in the lemon juice and salt to taste.

3 Purée the soup in batches in a blender or food processor. Return the soup to the pot, add the spice mixture and the remaining stock or water and simmer for 10 minutes.

4 Add the milk, taste and adjust the seasoning, if necessary. Stir in the chopped cilantro and reheat gently. Serve hot, with a swirl of yogurt.

VARIATION

As this soup has quite a hot and spicy flavor, it may be wise to omit or at least reduce the amount of chili in the recipe when serving it to children. A spoonful of plain yogurt, swirled into each serving of soup makes it extra nutritious and delicious.

STEP 1a

STEP 2

STEP 3

STEP 4

SPICED CORN & NUT MIX

A flavorful mixture of buttery-spiced nuts, raisins and popcorn to enjoy as a snack or with pre-dinner drinks.

SERVES 6

2 tbsp vegetable oil
¹/₄ cup popping corn
¹/₄ cup butter
1 garlic clove, peeled and crushed
¹/₃ cup unblanched almonds
¹/₂ cup unsalted cashews
¹/₂ cup unsalted peanuts
1 tsp Worcestershire sauce
1 tsp curry powder or paste
¹/₄ tsp chili powder
¹/₃ cup seedless raisins
salt

1 Heat the oil in a saucepan. Add the popping corn, stir well, then cover and cook over a fairly high heat for 3-5 minutes, holding the saucepan lid firmly and shaking the pan frequently until the popping stops.

2 Turn the popped corn into a dish, discarding any unpopped corn kernels.

3 Melt the butter in a skillet, add the garlic, almonds, cashews and peanuts, then stir in the Worcestershire sauce, curry powder or paste and chili powder and cook over medium heat for 2-3 minutes, stirring frequently.

4 Remove the skillet from the heat and stir in the raisins and popped corn. Season with salt to taste and mix well. Transfer to a serving bowl and serve warm or cold.

VARIATIONS

Use a mixture of any unsalted nuts of your choice – walnuts, pecans, hazelnuts, Brazil nuts, macadamia nuts and pine nuts are all delicious prepared this way. For a less fiery flavor omit the curry powder and chili powder and add 1 tsp cumin seeds, 1 tsp ground cilantro and ½ tsp paprika. Sprinkle with 1-2 tbsp of chopped fresh cilantro just before serving.

STEP 1

STEP 2

STEP 3

STEP 4

GARLICKY MUSHROOM PAKORAS

Whole mushrooms are dunked in a spiced garlicky batter and deep-fried until golden. They are at their most delicious served hot and freshly cooked.

SERVES 6

1¹/₂ cups gram flour (see box)
¹/₂ tsp salt
¹/₄ tsp baking powder
1 tsp cumin seeds
¹/₂-1 tsp chili powder, to taste
³/₄ cup water
2 garlic cloves, peeled and crushed
1 small onion, peeled and finely chopped
vegetable oil, for deep-frying
1 lb button mushrooms, trimmed and wiped
kosher salt, to serve
lemon wedges and cilantro sprigs, to garnish

1 Put the gram flour, salt, baking powder, cumin and chili powder into a bowl and mix well together. Make a well in the center of the mixture and gradually stir in the water, mixing to form a batter.

2 Stir the crushed garlic and the chopped onion into the batter and leave the mixture to infuse for 10 minutes. One-third fill a deep-fat fryer or pan with vegetable oil and heat to 350°F or until hot enough to brown a cube of day-old bread in 30 seconds. Lower the basket into the hot oil.

3 Meanwhile, mix the mushrooms into the batter, stirring to coat. Remove a few at a time and place them into the hot oil. Fry for about 2 minutes or until golden brown.

4 Remove from the pot with a slotted spoon and drain on paper towels while cooking the remainder in the same way. Serve hot, sprinkled with kosher salt and garnished with lemon wedges and cilantro sprigs.

GRAM FLOUR

Gram flour (also known as besan flour) is a pale yellow flour made from chick peas. It is now readily available from larger supermarkets as well as Indian food stores and some ethnic delicatessens. Gram flour is also used to make onion bhajis.

VEGETABLE & CASHEW SAMOSAS

These delicious little fried pastries are really quite simple to make.
Serve them hot as an appetizer to an Indian meal or cold as
a well-flavored picnic or lunch-box snack.

STEP 1

MAKES 12

2 cups potatoes, peeled and diced
salt
1 cup frozen peas
3 tbsp vegetable oil
1 onion, peeled and chopped
1 in piece gingerroot, peeled and chopped
1 garlic clove, peeled and crushed
1 tsp garam masala
2 tsp mild curry paste
1/2 tsp cumin seeds
2 tsp lemon juice
1/2 cup unsalted cashews, coarsely chopped
vegetable oil, for shallow frying
cilantro sprigs, to garnish
mango chutney, to serve

PASTRY:
2 cups all-purpose flour
1/4 cup butter, diced
6 tbsp warm milk

STEP 2

1 Cook the potatoes in a saucepan of boiling, salted water for 5 minutes. Add the peas and cook for a further 4 minutes or until the potato is tender. Drain well. Heat the oil in a skillet, add the onion, potato and pea mixture, ginger, garlic and spices and fry for 2 minutes. Stir in the lemon juice and cook gently, uncovered, for 2 minutes. Remove from the heat, slightly mash the potato and peas, then add the cashews, mix well and season with salt.

2 To make the dough, put the flour in a bowl and rub in the butter finely. Mix in the milk to form a dough. Knead lightly and divide into 6 portions. Form each into a ball and roll out on a lightly floured surface to a 7-in circle. Cut each one in half.

3 Divide the filling equally between each semicircle of dough, spreading it out to within ¼ in of the edges. Brush the edges of dough all the way around with water and fold over to form triangular shapes, sealing the edges well together to enclose the filling completely.

STEP 3

4 One-third fill a large, deep skillet with oil and heat to 350°F or until hot enough to brown a cube of bread in 30 seconds. Fry the samosas, a few at a time, turning frequently until golden brown and heated through. Drain on paper towels and keep warm while cooking the remainder in the same way. Garnish with cilantro sprigs and serve hot.

STEP 4

CHAPTER TWO

Main Dishes

India has long stood as the undisputed centre of vegetarianism. This is partly due to religious reasons (Hindus are forbidden meat), and partly due to economic factors. The vegetarian dishes they eat therefore supply all the proteins, vitamins and minerals that the human body needs.

The Indians make great use and show creative flair in using their staples of rice, lentils, fruit, nuts, eggs, milk, legumes and vegetables to make a seemingly endless array of dishes from biryanis and curries to pilaus and paneers that delight the appetite.

Such basic foodstuffs are used to create spicy, wholesome curries; stuffed vegetable treats using eggplants and potatoes; rice and vegetable pilaus with crunchy nut crowns; and nut and lentil "meatballs" better known as koftas. Mixed and matched with flavorsome rice, lentil, vegetable and bread accompaniments, they make a nutritious feast for the vegetarian.

Opposite: Plowing a rice paddy with the help of water buffaloes, near Madras.

STEP 1

STEP 2

STEP 3

STEP 4

EGG & LENTIL CURRY

A nutritious meal that is easy and relatively quick to make. The curried lentil sauce is also delicious served with cooked vegetables such as cauliflower, potatoes or eggplants.

SERVES 4

3 tbsp ghee or vegetable oil
1 large onion, peeled and chopped
2 garlic cloves, peeled and chopped
1-in piece gingerroot, peeled and chopped
$\frac{1}{2}$ tsp minced chili (from a jar), or use
   chili powder
1 tsp ground cilantro
1 tsp ground cumin
1 tsp paprika
$\frac{1}{2}$ cup split red lentils
$1\frac{3}{4}$ cups vegetable stock
1 cup canned chopped tomatoes
6 eggs
$\frac{1}{4}$ cup coconut milk
salt
2 tomatoes, cut into wedges, and cilantro
   sprigs, to garnish
parathas, chapatis or naan bread, to serve

1 Heat the ghee or oil in a saucepan, add the onion and fry gently for 3 minutes. Stir in the garlic, ginger, chili and spices and cook gently for 1 minute, stirring frequently. Stir in the lentils, stock and chopped tomatoes and bring to a boil. Reduce the heat, cover and simmer gently for 30 minutes, stirring occasionally until the lentils and onion are tender.

2 Meanwhile, place the eggs in a seperate pot of cold water and bring to a boil. Reduce the heat and simmer for 10 minutes. Drain and cover immediately with cold water.

3 Stir the coconut milk into the lentil mixture and season well with salt to taste. Purée the mixture in a blender or food processor until smooth. Return to the pot and heat through.

4 Shell and cut the hard-boiled eggs in half lengthwise. Arrange 3 halves, in a petal design, on each serving plate. Spoon the hot lentil sauce over the eggs, adding enough to flood the serving plate. Arrange a tomato wedge and a cilantro sprig between each halved egg. Serve hot with parathas, chapatis or naan bread to mop up the sauce.

COOK'S NOTE

Eggs contain high quality protein, fat, iron, and Vitamins A, B and D, although they are also high in cholesterol. Incidentally, a brown-shelled egg and a rich yellow yolk has the same nutritional value as a white egg.

STEP 1

STEP 2

STEP 3

STEP 4

BROWN RICE WITH FRUIT & NUTS

Here is a delicious and filling rice dish that is nice and spicy and includes fruits for a refreshing flavor and toasted nuts for an interesting crunchy texture.

SERVES 4-6

4 tbsp ghee or vegetable oil
1 large onion, peeled and chopped
2 garlic cloves, peeled and crushed
1-in piece gingerroot, peeled and chopped
1 tsp chili powder
1 tsp cumin seeds
1 tbsp mild or medium curry powder or paste
1½ cups long-grain brown rice
3¾ cups boiling vegetable stock
1 x 14-oz can chopped tomatoes
salt and freshly ground black pepper
1½ cups ready-soaked dried apricots or
    peaches, cut into slivers
1 red bell pepper, cored, seeded and diced
¾ cup frozen peas
1-2 small, slightly green bananas
⅓-½ cup toasted nuts (a mixture of almonds,
    cashews and hazelnuts, or pine nuts)
cilantro sprigs, to garnish

1 Heat the ghee or oil in a large saucepan, add the onion and fry gently for 3 minutes. Stir in the garlic, ginger, spices and rice and cook gently for 2 minutes, stirring all the time until the rice is coated in the spiced oil.

2 Pour in the boiling stock and add the canned tomatoes and season with salt and pepper to taste. Bring to a boil, then reduce the heat, cover and simmer gently for 40 minutes or until the rice is almost cooked and most of the liquid is absorbed.

3 Add the slivered apricots or peaches, diced red bell pepper and peas. Cover and continue cooking for 10 minutes. Remove from the heat and allow to stand for 5 minutes without uncovering.

4 Peel and slice the bananas. Uncover the rice mixture and fork through to mix the ingredients together. Add the toasted nuts and sliced banana and toss lightly. Transfer to a warm serving platter and garnish with cilantro sprigs. Serve hot.

COOK'S NOTE

Brown rice has a delicious nutty flavor and a more chewy texture than white rice. And because the germ of the grain is retained, it also contains larger amounts of vitamins, minerals and protein. Brown rice takes longer to cook than white rice.

MUTTAR PANEER

Paneer is a delicious fresh, soft cheese frequently used in Indian cooking. It is easily made at home, but remember to make it the day before required.

STEP 1

STEP 3

STEP 4a

STEP 4b

SERVES 6

$^2/_3$ cup vegetable oil
2 onions, peeled and chopped
2 garlic cloves, peeled and crushed
1-in piece gingerroot, peeled and chopped
1 tsp garam masala
1 tsp ground turmeric
1 tsp chili powder
3 cups frozen peas
1 cup canned chopped tomatoes
$^1/_2$ cup vegetable stock
salt and freshly ground black pepper
2 tbsp chopped fresh cilantro

PANEER:

2 $^1/_2$ quarts whole milk
5 tbsp lemon juice
1 garlic clove, peeled and crushed (optional)
1 tbsp chopped fresh cilantro (optional)

1 Bring the milk to a rolling boil in a large saucepan. Remove from the heat and stir in the lemon juice. Return to the heat for about 1 minute until the curds and whey separate. Remove from the heat. Line a colander with double thickness cheesecloth and pour the mixture through the cheesecloth, adding the garlic and cilantro, if using. Squeeze all the liquid from the curds and leave to drain.

2 Transfer to a dish, cover with a plate and weights and leave overnight in the refrigerator.

3 Cut the pressed paneer into small cubes. Heat the oil in a large skillet, add the paneer cubes and fry until golden on all sides. Remove from the pan and drain on paper towels.

4 Pour off some of the oil, leaving about 4 tablespoons in the skillet. Add the onions, garlic and ginger and fry gently for about 5 minutes, stirring frequently. Stir in the spices and fry gently for 2 minutes. Add the peas, tomatoes and stock and season with salt and pepper. Cover and simmer for 10 minutes, stirring occasionally, until the onion is tender. Add the fried paneer cubes and cook for a further 5 minutes. Taste and adjust the seasoning, if necessary. Sprinkle with the cilantro and serve at once.

SPLIT PEAS WITH VEGETABLES

Here is a simple, yet nourishing and flavorful way of cooking yellow split peas. Vary the selection of vegetables and spices according to personal preferences.

STEP 2

STEP 3

STEP 4

STEP 5

SERVES 4-5

1¹⁄₃ cup dried yellow split peas
5 cups cold water
¹⁄₂ tsp ground turmeric (optional)
1 lb new potatoes, scrubbed
5 tbsp vegetable oil
2 onions, peeled and coarsely chopped
2 ¹⁄₂ cups button mushrooms, wiped
1 tsp ground cilantro
1 tsp ground cumin
1 tsp chili powder
1 tsp garam masala
salt and freshly ground black pepper
1³⁄₄ cups vegetable stock
¹⁄₂ cauliflower, broken into flowerets
²⁄₃ cup frozen peas
6 oz cherry tomatoes
halved mint sprigs, to garnish

1 Place the split peas in a bowl, add the cold water and leave to soak for at least 4 hours or overnight.

2 Place the peas and the soaking liquid in a fairly large saucepan, stir in the turmeric, if using, and bring to a boil. Skim off any surface scum, half-cover the pan with a lid and simmer gently for 20 minutes or until the peas are tender and almost dry. Remove the pot from the heat and reserve.

3 Meanwhile, cut the potatoes into ¼-in slices. Heat the oil in a flameproof casserole, add the onions, potatoes and mushrooms and cook gently for 5 minutes, stirring frequently. Stir in the spices and fry gently for 1 minute, then add salt and pepper to taste, stock and cauliflower flowerets.

4 Cover and simmer gently for 25 minutes or until the potato is tender, stirring occasionally. Add the split peas (and any of the cooking liquid) and the frozen peas. Bring to a boil, cover and continue cooking for 5 minutes.

5 Stir in the halved cherry tomatoes and cook for 2 minutes. Taste and adjust the seasoning, if necessary. Serve hot, garnished with mint sprigs.

VARIATION

Chana dal (popular with vegetarians because of its high-protein content) may be used instead of yellow split peas, if preferred. *Chana dal* is similar to yellow split peas, although the grains are smaller and the flavor sweeter.

STUFFED EGGPLANTS

*These are delicious served hot or cold, topped with plain yogurt
or cucumber and yogurt combined.*

STEP 1

STEP 2

STEP 3

STEP 4

SERVES 6
OVEN: 350°F

1⅓ cups ⸳⸳⸳ nental lentils
3¾ cup⸳⸳⸳ ⸳r
2 garlic cloves, peeled and crushed
3 well-shaped eggplants, leaf ends trimmed
⅔ cup vegetable oil
salt and freshly ground black pepper
2 onions, peeled and chopped
4 tomatoes, chopped
2 tsp cumin seeds
1 tsp ground cinnamon
2 tbsp mild curry paste
1 tsp minced chili (from a jar)
2 tbsp chopped fresh mint
plain yogurt and mint sprigs, to serve

1 Rinse the lentils under cold
running water. Drain and place in
a saucepan with the water and garlic.
Cover and simmer for 30 minutes.

2 Cook the eggplants in a separate
pot of boiling water for 5 minutes.
Drain, then plunge into cold water for 5
minutes. Drain again, then cut the
eggplants in half lengthwise and scoop
out most of the flesh and reserve, leaving
a ½-in thick border to form a shell.

3 Place the eggplant shells in a
shallow greased ovenproof dish,
brush with a little oil and sprinkle with
salt and pepper. Cook in the preheated
oven for 10 minutes. Meanwhile, heat
half the remaining oil in a skillet, add the
onions and tomatoes and fry gently for 5
minutes. Chop the reserved eggplant
flesh, add to the skillet with the spices
and cook gently for 5 minutes. Season
with salt.

4 Stir in the lentils, most of the
remaining oil, reserving a little, and
the mint. Spoon the mixture into the
shells. Drizzle with remaining oil and
bake for 15 minutes. Serve hot or cold
topped with a spoonful of plain yogurt
and mint sprigs.

COOK'S TIP

Choose nice plump eggplants rather than
thin tapering ones because they retain
their shape better when baked with a
stuffing.

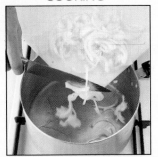

STEP 1a

STEP 1b

STEP 2

STEP 3

LENTIL & VEGETABLE BIRYANI

The delicious mix of vegetables, basmati rice and lentils produces this wholesome and nutritious dish.

SERVES 6

²/₃ cup lentils
4 tbsp ghee or vegetable oil
2 onions, peeled, quartered and sliced
2 garlic cloves, peeled and crushed
1 in piece gingerroot, peeled and chopped
1 tsp ground turmeric
¹/₂ tsp chili powder
1 tsp ground cilantro
2 tsp ground cumin
3 tomatoes, skinned and chopped
1 eggplant trimmed, and cut in ¹/₂-in pieces
6¹/₄ cups boiling vegetable stock
1 red or green bell pepper, cored, seeded and diced
1³/₄ cups basmati rice
1 cup thin green beans, topped, tailed and halved
1¹/₃ cups cauliflower flowerets
1¹/₂ cups mushrooms, wiped and sliced or quartered
¹/₂ cup unsalted cashews
3 hard-boiled eggs, shelled, to garnish
cilantro sprigs, to garnish

1 Rinse the lentils under cold running water and drain. Heat the ghee or oil in a saucepan, add the onions and fry gently for 2 minutes. Stir in the garlic, ginger and spices and fry gently for 1 minute, stirring frequently. Add the lentils, tomatoes, eggplant and 2 ½ cups of the stock, mix well, then cover and simmer gently for 20 minutes. Add the red or green bell pepper and cook for a further 10 minutes or until the lentils are tender and all the liquid has been absorbed.

2 Meanwhile, place the rice in a strainer and rinse under cold running water until the water runs clear. Drain and place in another pot with the remaining stock. Bring to a boil, add the green beans, cauliflower and mushrooms, then cover and cook gently for 15 minutes or until rice and vegetables are tender. Remove from the heat and leave, covered, for 10 minutes.

3 Add the lentil mixture and the cashews to the cooked rice and mix lightly together. Pile onto a warm serving platter and garnish with wedges of hard-boiled egg and cilantro sprigs. Serve hot.

STEP 1

STEP 2

STEP 3a

STEP 3b

BAKED POTATOES WITH BEANS

*Baked potatoes, topped with a mixture of beans in a
spicy sauce, provide a deliciously filling, high-fiber dish.*

SERVES 6
OVEN: 400°F

6 large baking potatoes
4 tbsp vegetable ghee or oil
1 large onion, peeled and chopped
2 garlic cloves, peeled and crushed
1 tsp ground turmeric
1 tbsp cumin seeds
2 tbsp mild or medium curry paste
12 oz cherry tomatoes
1 x 14-oz can black-eye peas, drained and
    rinsed
1 x 14-oz can red kidney beans, drained and
    rinsed
1 tbsp lemon juice
2 tbsp tomato paste
$^2/_3$ cup water
2 tbsp chopped fresh mint or cilantro
salt and freshly ground black pepper
plain yogurt, to serve
mint or cilantro sprigs, to garnish

1 Wash and scrub the potatoes and
prick several times with a fork.
Place in the oven and bake for 1-1¼
hours or until the potatoes feel soft when
gently squeezed.

2 About 20 minutes before the end of
cooking time, prepare the topping.
Heat the ghee or oil in a saucepan, add

the onion and cook gently for 5 minutes,
stirring frequently. Add the garlic,
turmeric, cumin seeds and curry paste
and cook gently for 1 minute. Stir in the
tomatoes, black-eye peas and red kidney
beans, lemon juice, tomato paste, water
and chopped mint or cilantro. Season
with salt and pepper, then cover and
cook gently for 10 minutes, stirring
frequently.

3 When the potatoes are cooked, cut
them in half and mash the flesh
lightly with a fork. Spoon the prepared
bean mixture on top, garnish with mint
or cilantro sprigs and serve with a dish of
plain yogurt.

VARIATION

Instead of cutting the potatoes in half, cut
a cross in each and squeeze gently to
open out. Spoon some of the prepared
filling into the cross and place any
remaining filling on the side.

STEP 1

STEP 2

STEP 3

STEP 3b

SPINACH & EGGPLANT

This interesting combination of lentils and spiced vegetables is delicious served with parathas, chapatis or naan bread, plus a bowl of plain yogurt.

SERVES 4

1¹/₃ cup split red lentils
3 cups water
1 onion
1 eggplant
1 red bell pepper
2 zucchini
4 oz mushrooms, wiped
¹/₂ lb leaf spinach
4 tbsp vegetable ghee or oil
1 fresh green chili, seeded and chopped, or
    use 1 tsp minced chili (from a jar)
1 tsp ground cumin
1 tsp ground cilantro
1-in piece gingerroot, peeled and chopped
²/₃ cup vegetable stock
salt
cilantro or flat-leaved parsley sprigs, to
    garnish

1 Wash the lentils and place in a saucepan with the water. Cover and simmer for 15 minutes until the lentils are soft but still whole.

2 Meanwhile, peel, quarter and slice the onion. Trim leaf end and cut the eggplant into ½-in pieces. Remove stem end and seeds from the bell pepper and cut into ½-in pieces. Trim and cut zucchini into ½-in thick slices. Thickly slice the mushrooms. Discard coarse stems from spinach leaves and wash spinach well.

3 Heat the ghee or oil in a large saucepan, add the onion and red bell pepper and fry gently for 3 minutes, stirring frequently. Stir in the eggplant, mushrooms, chili, spices and ginger and fry gently for 1 minute. Add the spinach and stock and season with salt to taste. Stir until the spinach leaves wilt down. Cover and simmer for 10 minutes or until the vegetables are just tender.

4 Make a border of the lentils on a warm serving plate and spoon the vegetable mixture into the center. (The lentils may be stirred into the vegetable mixture, instead of being used as a border, if wished.) Garnish with cilantro or flat-leaved parsley sprigs.

SPINACH

Wash the spinach thoroughly in several changes of cold water because it can be gritty. Drain well and shake off excess water from leaves before adding to the pot.

STEP 2

STEP 3

STEP 4

STEP 5

VEGETABLE, NUT & LENTIL KOFTAS

This mixture is shaped into golf-ball shapes and baked in the oven with a sprinkling of aromatic garam masala. These are delicious served hot or cold with a yogurt dressing and chapatis.

SERVES 4-5
OVEN: 350°F

6 tbsp vegetable ghee or oil
1 onion, peeled and finely chopped
2 carrots, peeled and finely chopped
2 celery stalks, trimmed and finely chopped
2 garlic cloves, peeled and crushed
1 fresh green chili, seeded and finely
  chopped
1½ tbsp curry powder or paste
1⅓ cups split red lentils
2½ cups vegetable stock
2 tbsp tomato paste
2 cups fresh whole-wheat bread crumbs
¾ cup unsalted cashews, finely chopped
2 tbsp chopped fresh cilantro or parsley
1 egg, beaten
salt and freshly ground black pepper
garam masala, for sprinkling

YOGURT DRESSING:
1 cup plain yogurt
1-2 tbsp chopped fresh cilantro or parsley
1-2 tbsp mango chutney, chopped if
  necessary

1 Heat 4 tablespoons of ghee or oil in a large saucepan and gently fry the onion, carrots, celery, garlic and chili for 5 minutes, stirring frequently. Add the

curry powder or paste and the lentils and cook gently for 1 minute, stirring.

2 Add the stock and tomato paste and bring to a boil. Reduce the heat, cover and simmer for 20 minutes or until the lentils are tender and all the liquid is absorbed.

3 Remove from the heat and cool slightly. Add the bread crumbs, nuts, cilantro, egg and seasoning to taste. Mix well and leave to cool. Shape into balls about the size of golf balls. (The mixture is quite soft, so use 2 spoons to help shape the balls, if necessary.)

4 Place the balls on a greased baking sheet, drizzle with the remaining oil and sprinkle with a little garam masala, to taste. Cook in the preheated oven for 15-20 minutes or until piping hot and lightly golden.

5 Meanwhile, make the yogurt dressing. Mix all the ingredients together in a bowl. Serve the koftas hot with the yogurt dressing.

CHICK-PEAS & EGGPLANT

*Canned chick-peas (widely available from supermarkets) are used in
this dish, but you can use black-eye peas or red kidney beans
if you prefer. Omit the chilies for a less fiery flavour.*

STEP 1a

SERVES 4

1 large eggplant
2 zucchini
6 tbsp ghee or vegetable oil
1 large onion, peeled, quartered and sliced
2 garlic cloves, peeled and crushed
1-2 fresh green chilies, seeded and chopped,
   or use 1-2 tsp minced chili (from a jar)
2 tsp ground cilantro
2 tsp cumin seeds
1 tsp ground turmeric
1 tsp garam masala
1 x 14-oz can chopped tomatoes
1¼ cups vegetable stock or water
salt and freshly ground black pepper
1 x 14-oz can chick-peas, drained and rinsed
2 tbsp chopped fresh mint
²/₃ cup heavy cream

STEP 1b

1 Trim the leaf end off the eggplant
and cut into cubes. Trim and slice
the zucchini. Heat the ghee or oil in a
saucepan and gently fry the eggplant,
zucchini, onion, garlic and chilies for
about 5 minutes, stirring frequently and
adding a little more oil to the pan, if
necessary.

2 Stir in the spices and cook for 30
seconds. Add the tomatoes, stock
and salt and pepper to taste and cook for
10 minutes.

3 Add the chick-peas to the pot and
continue cooking for a further 5
minutes. Stir in the mint and cream and
reheat gently. Taste and adjust the
seasoning, if necessary. Serve hot with
plain or pilau rice, or with parathas, if
preferred.

STEP 2

YOGURT

You could use plain yogurt instead of
cream in this dish, in which case first
blend it with ½ tsp cornstarch before
adding to the pot and heating gently,
stirring constanty. The cornstarch helps
stabilize the yogurt to prevent it from
separating during heating.

STEP 3

STEP 1

STEP 2

STEP 3

STEP 4

VEGETABLE CURRY

This colorful and interesting mixture of vegetables, cooked in a spicy sauce, is excellent served with pilau rice and naan bread. Vary the vegetables according to personal preferences.

SERVES 4

*¹/₂ lb turnips or rutabaga, peeled
1 eggplant, leaf end trimmed
12 oz new potatoes, scrubbed
¹/₂ lb cauliflower
3 ¹/₂ cups button mushrooms, wiped
1 large onion, peeled
¹/₂ lb carrots, peeled
6 tbsp ghee or vegetable oil
2 garlic cloves, peeled and crushed
2-in piece gingerroot, peeled and chopped
1-2 fresh green chilies, seeded and chopped
1 tbsp paprika
2 tsp ground cilantro
1 tbsp mild or medium curry powder or
    paste
1³/₄ cups vegetable stock
1 x 14-oz can chopped tomatoes
salt
1 green bell pepper, seeded and sliced
1 tbsp cornstarch
²/₃ cup coconut milk
2-3 tbsp blanched almonds, finely ground
cilantro sprigs, to garnish*

1 Cut the turnips or rutabaga, eggplant and potatoes into ½-in cubes. Divide the cauliflower into small flowerets. Leave the mushrooms whole, or slice thickly, if preferred. Slice the onion and carrots.

2 Heat the ghee or oil in a large saucepan, add the onion, turnip, potato and cauliflower and cook gently for 3 minutes, stirring frequently. Add the garlic, ginger, chili, spices and curry powder or paste and cook for 1 minute, stirring.

3 Add the stock, tomatoes, eggplant and mushrooms and season with salt. Cover and simmer gently for about 30 minutes, or until tender, stirring occasionally. Add the green bell pepper, cover and continue cooking for a further 5 minutes.

4 Smoothly blend the cornstarch with the coconut milk and stir into the mixture. Add the ground almonds and simmer for 2 minutes, stirring all the time. Taste and adjust the seasoning, if necessary. Serve hot, garnished with cilantro sprigs.

GROUND ALMONDS

The ground almonds used in this dish not only help to thicken the sauce but also add richness and flavor to it. For a less fiery flavor in the dish, reduce or omit the amount of chili used.

STEP 1

STEP 2

STEP 3

STEP 4

SPICED BASMATI PILAU

Omit the broccoli and mushrooms from this recipe if you require only a simple spiced pilau. The whole spices are not meant to be eaten and may be removed before serving, if wished.

SERVES 6

2¹/₂ cups basmati rice
6 oz broccoli, trimmed
6 tbsp vegetable oil
2 large onions, peeled and chopped
3 ¹/₂ cups mushrooms, wiped and sliced
2 garlic cloves, peeled and crushed
6 cardamom pods, split
6 whole cloves
8 black peppercorns
1 cinnamon stick or piece of cassia bark
1 tsp ground turmeric
5 cups boiling vegetable stock or water
salt and freshly ground black pepper
¹/₃ cup seedless raisins
¹/₂ cup unsalted pistachios, coarsely chopped

1 Place the rice in a strainer and wash well under cold running water until the water runs clear. Drain. Trim off most of the broccoli stem and cut into small flowerets, then quarter the stem lengthwise and cut diagonally into ½-in pieces.

2 Heat the oil in a large saucepan, add the onions and broccoli stems and cook gently for 3 minutes, stirring frequently. Add the mushrooms, rice, garlic and spices and cook gently for 1 minute, stirring frequently until the rice is coated in spiced oil.

3 Add the boiling stock and season with salt and pepper. Stir in the broccoli flowerets and return the mixture to a boil. Cover, reduce the heat and cook gently for 15 minutes without uncovering.

4 Remove from the heat and leave to stand for 5 minutes without uncovering. Add the raisins and pistachios and gently fork through to fluff up the grains. Serve hot.

VARIATION

For added richness, you could stir a spoonful of vegetable ghee through the rice mixture just before serving. A little diced red pepper and a few cooked peas or corn kernels forked through at step 4 add a colorful touch.

CHAPTER THREE

Accompaniments

Bread accompanies nearly every meal in the form of parathas, which are basically fried chapattis; Naan, or leavened baked bread; crisp and crunchy poppadoms, flavoured or plain; and puris, small rounds of deep-fried bread that are sometimes stuffed with savory ingredients.

Vegetable accompaniments come in all guises, as mixed curried dishes; as fritters, delicious with a spoonful of relish; and as bhajis, which are basically fried and spiced vegetables. They all contribute to give an Indian meal flavor and texture as well as extra nourishment.

Needless to say rice is a staple food and is served as a matter of course with virtually every meal. Experiment by cooking it in a little coconut milk with just a pinch of spices or garam masala to liven up plain boiled or steamed rice. Also consider serving spiced potatoes and cooked lentils as an alternative to rice – they make a welcome change and provide good nutrition.

Opposite: *A spice market in India.*

CURRIED OKRA

Okra, also known as bhindi and lady's fingers, are a favorite Indian vegetable. You can buy them in many supermarkets, as well as Asian food stores and specialist vegetable stores.

STEP 1

STEP 2a

STEP 2b

STEP 3

SERVES 4

1 lb fresh okra
4 tbsp ghee or vegetable oil
1 bunch scallions, trimmed and sliced
2 garlic cloves, peeled and crushed
2 in piece gingerroot, peeled and chopped
1 tsp minced chili (from a jar)
1½ tsp ground cumin
1 tsp ground cilantro
1 tsp ground turmeric
1 cup canned chopped tomatoes
⅔ cup vegetable stock
salt and freshly ground black pepper
1 tsp garam masala
chopped fresh cilantro, to garnish

1 Wash the okra, trim off the stems and pat dry. Heat the ghee or oil in a large saucepan, add the scallions, garlic, ginger and chili and fry gently for 1 minute, stirring frequently.

2 Stir in the spices and fry gently for 30 seconds, then add the tomatoes, stock and okra. Season with salt and pepper to taste and simmer for about 15 minutes, stirring and turning the mixture occasionally. The okra should be cooked but still a little crisp.

3 Sprinkle with the garam masala, taste and adjust the seasoning, if necessary. Garnish with the chopped cilantro and serve hot.

COOK'S TIP

If preferred, slice the okra into rings, add to the mixture (step 2), cover and cook until tender-crisp, stirring occasionally. When you buy fresh okra, make sure the pods are not shriveled and that they do not have any brown spots. Once you get it home, it will keep for 3 days tightly wrapped in the refrigerator.

EGGPLANT IN SAFFRON SAUCE

*Here is a quick and simple, delicately spiced and delicious
way to cook eggplant.*

SERVES 4

a good pinch of saffron strands, finely
  crushed
1 tbsp boiling water
1 large eggplant
3 tbsp vegetable oil
1 large onion, peeled and coarsely chopped
2 garlic cloves, peeled and crushed
1-in piece gingerroot, peeled and chopped
1¹/₂ tbsp mild or medium curry paste
1 tsp cumin seeds
²/₃ cup heavy cream
²/₃ cup plain yogurt
2 tbsp mango chutney, chopped if necessary
salt and freshly ground black pepper

1 Place the saffron in a small bowl,
add the boiling water and leave to
infuse for 5 minutes. Trim the leaf end off
the eggplant, cut lengthwise into
quarters, then into ½-in thick slices.

2 Heat the oil in a large skillet, add
the onion and cook gently for 3
minutes. Stir in the eggplant, garlic,
ginger, curry paste and cumin and cook
gently for 3 minutes.

3 Stir in the saffron water, cream,
yogurt and chutney and cook

gently for 8-10 minutes, stirring
frequently, until the eggplant is cooked
through and tender. Season with salt and
pepper to taste and serve hot.

> ### YOGURT
>
> You will find that yogurt adds a creamy
> texture and pleasant tartness to this sauce.
> If you are worried about it separating
> when heated, add a tablespoonful at a
> time and stir it in well before adding
> another. A little cornstarch blended with
> the yogurt before cooking, also helps
> prevent it from separating when heated.

STEP 1a

STEP 1b

STEP 2

STEP 3

SPINACH & CAULIFLOWER BHAJI

*This excellent vegetable dish goes well with most Indian food –
and it is simple and quick cooking, too.*

SERVES 4

1 cauliflower
1 lb fresh spinach, washed, or 8 oz frozen
    spinach, defrosted
4 tbsp ghee or vegetable oil
2 large onions, peeled and coarsely chopped
2 garlic cloves, peeled and crushed
1-in piece gingerroot, peeled and chopped
1¼ tsp cayenne pepper, or to taste
1 tsp ground cumin
1 tsp ground turmeric
2 tsp ground cilantro
1 x 14-oz can chopped tomatoes
1¼ cups vegetable stock
salt and freshly ground black pepper

1 Divide the cauliflower into small
flowerets, discarding the hard
central core. Trim the stems from
spinach leaves. Heat the ghee or oil in a
large saucepan, add the onions and
cauliflower flowerets and fry the
vegetables gently for about 3 minutes,
stirring frequently.

2 Add the garlic, ginger and spices
and cook gently for 1 minute. Stir
in the tomatoes and the stock and season
with salt and pepper. Bring to a boil,
cover, reduce the heat and simmer gently
for 8 minutes.

3 Add the spinach to the pan,
stirring and turning to wilt the
leaves. Cover and simmer gently for
about 8-10 minutes, stirring frequently
until the spinach has wilted and the
cauliflower is tender. Serve hot.

SPINACH

You may prefer to use frozen spinach in
this recipe, in which case you require
½ lb frozen leaf spinach which must be
defrosted and well drained before adding
to the mixture and heating through.

FRIED SPICED POTATOES

Deliciously good and a super accompaniment to almost any main course dish, although rather high in calories!

STEP 1

SERVES 4-6

2 onions, peeled and quartered
2-in piece gingerroot, peeled and finely
    chopped
2 garlic cloves, peeled
2-3 tbsp mild or medium curry paste
4 tbsp water
1½ lb new potatoes
vegetable oil, for deep frying
3 tbsp vegetable ghee or oil
⅔ cup plain yogurt
⅔ cup heavy cream
3 tbsp chopped fresh mint
salt and freshly ground black pepper
½ bunch scallions, trimmed and chopped, to
    garnish

1 Place the onions, ginger, garlic, curry paste and water in a blender or food processor and process until smooth, scraping down the sides of machine and blending again, if necessary.

2 Cut the potatoes into quarters – the pieces need to be about 1 in in size – and pat dry with paper towels. Heat the oil in a deep-fat fryer to 350°F and fry the potatoes, in batches, for about 5 minutes or until golden brown, turning

frequently. Remove from the pan and drain on paper towels.

3 Heat the ghee or oil in a large skillet, add the curry and onion mixture and fry gently for 2 minutes, stirring all the time. Add the yogurt, cream and 2 tablespoons of mint and mix well.

4 Add the fried potatoes and stir until coated in the sauce. Cook for a further 5-7 minutes or until heated through and sauce has thickened, stirring frequently. Season with salt and pepper to taste and sprinkle with the remaining mint and sliced scallions. Serve immediately.

STEP 2

STEP 3

STEP 4

STEP 1

STEP 2

STEP 3

STEP 5

MIXED BELL PEPPER POORIS

Whole-wheat pooris are easy to make and so good to eat served with a topping of spicy mixed bell peppers and yogurt. You may, of course, simply make the pooris to serve plain with other dishes, if wished.

SERVES 6

POORIS:
1 cup whole-wheat flour
1 tbsp ghee or vegetable oil
2 good pinches of salt
$\frac{1}{3}$ cup hot water
vegetable oil, for shallow frying
plain yogurt, to serve
cilantro sprigs, to garnish

TOPPING:
4 tbsp vegetable ghee or oil
1 large onion, peeled, quartered and thinly
   sliced
$\frac{1}{2}$ red bell pepper, seeded and thinly sliced
$\frac{1}{2}$ green bell pepper, seeded and thinly sliced
$\frac{1}{4}$ eggplant, cut lengthwise into 6 wedges
   and thinly sliced
1 garlic clove, peeled and crushed
1 in piece gingerroot, peeled and chopped
$\frac{1}{2}$-1 tsp minced chili (from a jar)
2 tsp mild or medium curry paste
1 cup canned chopped tomatoes
salt

1 To make the pooris, put the flour in a bowl with the ghee or oil and salt. Add hot water and mix to form a fairly soft dough. Knead gently, cover with a damp cloth and leave for 30 minutes.

2 Meanwhile, prepare the topping. Heat the ghee or oil in a large saucepan, add the onion, bell peppers, eggplant, garlic, ginger, chili and curry paste and fry gently for 5 minutes. Stir in the tomatoes and salt to taste and simmer gently, uncovered, for 5 minutes, stirring occasionally until the sauce thickens. Remove from the heat.

3 Knead the dough on a floured surface and divide into 6. Roll each piece into a circle. Each circle should have a diameter of about 6-in. Cover each one as you finish rolling, to prevent it from drying out.

4 Heat about $\frac{1}{2}$ in oil in a large skillet. Add a poori, one at a time, and fry for about 15 seconds on each side until puffed and golden, turning frequently. Drain on paper towels and keep warm while cooking the remainder in the same way.

5 Reheat the vegetable mixture. Place a poori on each serving plate and top with the vegetable mixture. Add a spoonful of yogurt to each one and garnish with cilantro sprigs. Serve hot.

SWEET HOT CARROTS & BEANS

Take care not to overcook the vegetables in this tasty dish – they are definitely at their best served tender-crisp. Remember to discard the whole dried chilies before serving the dish.

STEP 1

STEP 2

STEP 3

STEP 4

SERVES 4

1 lb young carrots, trimmed and peeled if necessary
¹/₂ lb thin green beans
1 bunch scallions, trimmed
4 tbsp vegetable ghee or oil
1 tsp ground cumin
1 tsp ground cilantro
3 cardamom pods, split and seeds removed
2 whole dried red chilies
2 garlic cloves, peeled and crushed
1-2 tsp honey, to taste
1 tsp lime or lemon juice
salt and freshly ground black pepper
¹/₂ cup unsalted, toasted cashews
1 tbsp chopped fresh cilantro or parsley
slices of lime or lemon and cilantro sprigs, to garnish

1 Cut the carrots lengthwise into quarters and then in half crosswise if very long. Top and tail the beans. Cut the spring onions into 2-in pieces. Cook the carrots and beans in a saucepan containing a little boiling, salted water for 5-6 minutes according to how tender-crisp you like vegetables. Drain well.

2 Heat the ghee or oil in a large skillet, add the scallions, carrots, beans, cumin, cilantro, cardamom seeds and whole dried chilies. Cook gently for 2 minutes, stirring frequently.

3 Stir in the garlic, honey and lemon or lime juice and continue cooking for a further 2 minutes, stirring occasionally. Season to taste with salt and pepper. Remove and discard the whole chilies.

4 Sprinkle the vegetables with the toasted cashews and chopped cilantro, mix together lightly. Serve immediately, garnished with slices of lime or lemon and cilantro sprigs.

CARROTS

If the carrots are very slender, it may not be necessary to cut them into quarters. Simply trim the leafy ends, scrub well and cook in the boiling, salted water for a minute or two before adding the green beans to ensure all the vegetables cook evenly.

POTATO FRITTERS WITH RELISH

These are incredibly simple to make and sure to be popular served as a tempting snack or as an accompaniment to almost any Indian main course dish.

MAKES 8

$^{1}/_{2}$ cup whole-wheat flour
$^{1}/_{2}$ tsp ground cilantro
$^{1}/_{2}$ tsp cumin seeds
$^{1}/_{4}$ tsp chili powder
$^{1}/_{2}$ tsp ground turmeric
$^{1}/_{4}$ tsp salt
1 egg
3 tbsp milk
12 oz potatoes, peeled
1-2 garlic cloves, peeled and crushed
4 scallions, trimmed and chopped
$^{1}/_{2}$ cup whole-kernel corn
vegetable oil for shallow frying

ONION AND TOMATO RELISH:
1 onion, peeled
$^{1}/_{2}$ lb tomatoes
2 tbsp chopped fresh cilantro
2 tbsp chopped fresh mint
2 tbsp lemon juice
$^{1}/_{2}$ tsp roasted cumin seeds
$^{1}/_{4}$ tsp salt
a few pinches of cayenne pepper, to taste

1 First make the relish. Cut the onion and tomatoes into small dice and place in a bowl with the remaining ingredients. Mix together well and leave to stand for at least 15 minutes before

serving to allow time for the flavors to blend.

2 Place the flour in a bowl, stir in the spices and salt and make a well in the center. Add the egg and milk and mix to form a fairly thick batter.

3 Coarsely grate the potatoes, place in a strainer and rinse well under cold running water. Drain and squeeze dry, then stir into the batter with the garlic, scallions and corn.

4 Heat about ¼ in oil in a large skillet and add a few tablespoonfuls of the mixture at a time, flattening each one to form a thin cake. Fry gently for 2-3 minutes or until golden brown and cooked through, turning frequently.

5 Drain on paper towels and keep hot while frying the remaining mixture in the same way. Serve hot with onion and tomato relish.

PARATHAS

These triangular-shaped breads are so easy to make and are the perfect addition to most Indian meals. Serve hot, spread with a little butter, if wished.

STEP 1

MAKES 6

¾ cup all-purpose whole-wheat flour
¾ cup all-purpose white flour
a good pinch of salt
1 tbsp vegetable oil, plus extra for greasing
⅓ cup warm water

1 Place the flours and the salt in a bowl. Drizzle 1 tablespoon of oil over the flour, add the warm water and mix to form a soft dough, adding a little more water, if necessary. Knead on a lightly floured surface until smooth, then cover and leave for 30 minutes.

2 Knead the dough on a floured surface and divide into 6 equal pieces. Shape each one into a ball. Roll out on a floured surface into a 6-in circle and brush very lightly with oil.

3 Fold in half, and then in half again to form a triangle. Roll out to form a 7-in triangle (when measured from point to center top), dusting with extra flour as necessary.

4 Brush a large skillet with a little oil and heat until hot, then add one or two parathas and cook for about 1-1½ minutes. Brush the surfaces very lightly with oil, then turn and cook the other sides for 1½ minutes until cooked through.

5 Place the cooked parathas on a plate and cover with foil, or place between a clean dish towel to keep warm, while cooking the remainder in the same way, greasing the skillet between cooking each batch.

STEP 2

STEP 3

COOK'S TIP

If the parathas puff up a lot during cooking, press down lightly with a pancake turner. Make parathas in advance, if wished: wrap in foil and reheat in a hot oven for about 15 minutes when required.

STEP 4

CHAPTER FOUR

Desserts

The Indians frequently finish a meal with fresh fruit for dessert from the colorful supply available which includes mangoes, papayas, bananas, guavas and pears. Richer concoctions like carrot halva, mango ice cream, ice cool sherbets and saffron-scented rice pudding are served only on special occasions such as a religious festival. In India they would be served on the very finest tableware and decorated with *varq*, the edible silver or gold leaf.

Indian rice pudding is a true classic, but is cooked in a saucepan over a low heat rather than baked in the oven. It is very sweet, often saffron or rose-water scented and sprinkled with chopped nuts like pistachios. It is perhaps one of the most popular of all desserts made in Indian households. Other favorites like ice creams, coconut cream molds and halva also make great use of milk.

Do try some of these dishes, for it is true to say that Indian restaurants offer little in the way of special Indian desserts and they are always a pleasant and enjoyable taste experience.

Opposite: *Pavilions on Lake Gadsi-Sar, Rajastan.*

STEP 1

STEP 2

STEP 3

STEP 4

MANGO ICE CREAM

This delicious ice cream with its refreshing tang of mango and lime makes the perfect ending to a hot and spicy meal. You will find canned mango slices are widely available from larger supermarkets.

SERVES 4-6

²/₃ cup light cream
2 egg yolks
¹/₂ tsp cornstarch
1 tsp water
2 x 14-oz cans mango slices in syrup,
    drained
1 tbsp lime or lemon juice
²/₃ cup heavy cream
mint sprigs, to decorate

1 Heat the light cream in a saucepan until hot (but do not allow it to boil). Place the egg yolks in a bowl with the cornstarch and water and mix together until smooth. Pour the hot cream onto the egg yolk mixture, stirring all the time.

2 Return the mixture to the pan and place over a very low heat, beating or stirring all the time until the mixture thickens and coats the back of a wooden spoon. (Do not try and hurry this process or the mixture will overcook and spoil.) Pour into a bowl.

3 Purée the drained mango slices in a blender or food processor until smooth. Mix with the custard and stir in the lime juice. Whip the heavy cream until softly peaking and fold into the mango mixture until thoroughly combined.

4 Transfer the mixture to a bread pan or shallow freezerproof container. Cover and freeze for 2-3 hours, or until half-frozen and still mushy in the center. Turn the mixture into a bowl and mash well with a fork until smooth. Return to the container, cover and freeze again until firm.

5 Transfer the container of ice cream to the main compartment of the refrigerator for about 30 minutes before serving to allow it to soften slightly. Scoop or spoon the ice cream into serving dishes and decorate with mint sprigs.

ALTERNATIVE

Use the drained mango syrup for adding to fruit salads or for mixing into drinks.

SAFFRON-SPICED RICE PUDDING

This rich and comforting pudding is first cooked in milk delicately flavored with saffron and cinnamon. Raisins, dried apricots, almonds and cream are then added to the mixture before baking.

STEP 1

SERVES 4-5
OVEN: 325°F

2¹/₂ cups whole milk
several pinches of saffron strands, finely
    crushed (see below)
¹/₄ cup pudding rice
1 cinnamon stick or piece of cassia bark
3 tbsp granulated sugar
¹/₄ cup seedless raisins or golden raisins
¹/₄ cup ready-soaked dried apricots, chopped
1 egg, beaten
¹/₃ cup light cream
1 tbsp butter, diced
2 tbsp slivered almonds
freshly grated nutmeg, for sprinkling
cream, for serving (optional)

STEP 2a

3 Transfer the mixture to a greased baking dish or quiche dish, sprinkle with the almonds and freshly grated nutmeg, to taste. Bake in the preheated oven for 25-30 minutes until mixture is set and lightly golden. Serve hot with extra cream, if wished.

1 Place the milk and crushed saffron in a nonstick saucepan and bring to a boil. Stir in the rice and cinnamon stick, reduce the heat and simmer very gently, uncovered, for 25 minutes, stirring frequently until tender.

2 Remove the pot from the heat and discard the cinnamon stick from the rice mixture. Stir in the sugar, raisins and apricots, then beat in the egg, cream and diced butter.

STEP 2b

SAFFRON

For a slightly stronger saffron flavor, place the saffron strands on a small piece of kitchen foil and toast them lightly under a hot broiler for a few moments (take care not to overcook them or the flavor will spoil) and crush finely between fingers and thumb before adding to the milk.

STEP 3

STEP 1

STEP 2

STEP 3A

STEP 3B

COCONUT-CREAM MOLDS

Smooth, creamy and refreshing – these tempting little custards are made with an unusual combination of coconut milk, cream and eggs.

SERVES 8
OVEN: 275°F

CARAMEL:
½ cup granulated sugar
⅔ cup water

CUSTARD:
1¼ cups water
3 oz creamed coconut, chopped
2 eggs
2 egg yolks
1½ tbsp sugar
1¼ cups light cream
sliced banana or slivers of fresh pineapple
1-2 tbsp freshly grated or shredded coconut

1 Have ready 8 small ovenproof dishes, about ⅔-cup capacity. To make the caramel, place the sugar and water in a saucepan and heat gently to dissolve the sugar, then boil rapidly, without stirring, until the mixture turns a rich golden brown.

2 Remove at once from the heat and dip the base of the pot into a bowl of cold water (this stops it cooking). Quickly but carefully pour the caramel into the ovenproof dishes to coat the bases.

3 To make the custard, place the water in the same pot, add the coconut and heat until coconut dissolves, stirring all the time. Place the eggs, egg yolks and sugar in a bowl and beat well with a fork. Add the hot coconut milk and stir well to dissolve the sugar. Stir in the cream and strain mixture into a jug.

4 Arrange the dishes in a roasting pan and fill with enough cold water to come halfway up the sides of the dishes. Pour the custard mixture into the caramel-lined dishes, cover with foil and cook in the oven for about 40 minutes, or until set.

5 Remove the dishes from the roasting pan and leave to cool. Chill overnight in the refrigerator. To serve, run a knife around the edge of each dish and turn out onto a serving plate. Serve with slices of banana or slivers of fresh pineapple sprinkled with freshly grated or shredded coconut.

SWEET CARROT HALVA

*This nutritious dessert, made from grated carrots simmered in milk,
is flavored with spices, nuts and raisins. It is delicious served
plain or with heavy cream or yogurt.*

STEP 1a

STEP 1b

SERVES 6

3 cups carrots, peeled and grated
3 cups milk
1 cinnamon stick or piece of cassia bark
   (optional)
4 tbsp vegetable ghee or oil
¼ cup granulated sugar
¼ cup unsalted pistachio nuts, chopped
¼-½ cup blanched almonds, slivered or
   chopped
⅓ cup seedless raisins
8 cardamom pods, split and seeds removed
   and crushed
heavy cream or plain yogurt, to serve

3 Add the sugar, pistachios, almonds,
raisins and crushed cardamom
seeds, mix well and continue frying for a
further 3-4 minutes, stirring frequently.
Serve warm or cold with heavy cream or
yogurt.

1 Put the grated carrots, milk and
cinnamon or cassia, if using, into a
large, heavy-based saucepan and bring
to a boil. Reduce the heat to a simmer
and cook, uncovered, for 35-40 minutes,
or until the mixture is thick (with no milk
remaining). Stir the mixture frequently
during cooking to prevent it from
sticking.

2 Discard the cinnamon. Heat the
ghee or oil in a nonstick skillet, add
the carrot mixture and stir-fry over a
medium heat for about 5 minutes or
until the carrots take on a glossy sheen.

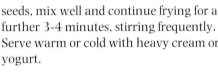

GRATING

The quickest and easiest way to grate this
quantity of carrots is by using a food
processor fitted with the appropriate
blade. This mixture may be prepared
ahead of time and reheated in the
microwave when required. Use green
cardamoms as these have the best flavor.

STEP 2

STEP 3

INDIAN VEGETARIAN COOKING

TASTY ACCOMPANIMENTS

Here is a selection of easy, delicious accompaniments to complement your Indian dishes.

Apple and onion relish Peel, core and coarsely grate 1 large cooking apple into a bowl. Add ½ bunch chopped scallions, 2 tsp vinegar or lemon juice, 1-2 tsp sugar, to taste, and ½ tsp roasted cumin seeds. Mix well and chill before serving, sprinkled with chopped fresh cilantro.

Radish and cucumber yogurt Put 2½ cups plain yogurt into a bowl and season with salt and freshly ground black pepper. Stir in ½ bunch trimmed and unpeeled, diced cucumber, 1 small chopped onion and 1-2 tbsp chopped fresh mint. Serve chilled.

Cucumber raita Mix 2½ cups plain yogurt with ½ peeled and grated cucumber. Season with salt, freshly ground black pepper and a pinch or two of cayenne pepper. Just before serving, dry roast 1 tsp cumin seeds, then crush coarsely and sprinkle over the yogurt mixture. Add a little finely chopped fresh mint to the mixture, if wished.

continued opposite

Here is a mouthwatering collection of easy Indian-style vegetarian recipes ranging from mild and fragrant, to hot and fiery, or simply nice and spicy. So whether you are looking for a simple nutritious snack, a substantial family meal or a special dish for entertaining, this book has a recipe to suit most palates and all occasions. You will find all the ingredients used here are available from larger supermarkets or Asian stores.

SPICES

It is well worth investing in some spices, to give authentic flavor to your Indian cooking. Here are just a few suggestions that will add variety and interest to all manner of dishes – from soups and appetizers to main courses, accompaniments and desserts.

Cardamom Small pods containing tiny black seeds with an aromatic flavour – green cardamoms are considered the best. These pods can be used whole or split (to fully appreciate the flavor from the seeds), or crushed and the seeds removed and used whole or ground, according to recipe requirements. The whole or split pods are not meant to be eaten and should be left on the side of the plate.

Cassia comes from the bark of the cassia tree and is not as attractive and uniform in shape as cinnamon, although the flavor is good, being stronger and less

delicate than cinnamon.

Cayenne pepper Orange-red in color, this ground pepper is extremely hot and pungent because it is made from dried red chilies. Not to be confused with paprika, which, although similar in color, is mild-flavored. Use caution with cayenne – a little goes a long way!

Chili powder Available in varying degrees of strength. Pure chili powder is extremely hot and should be used sparingly. It is best to check the label on jars before buying because many powders are a blend of chili and other spices and flavorings, and "chili seasoning" – a popular blend of spices – is quite mild.

Cilantro is available in seed or ground form and has a mild, spicy flavor with a slight orange-rind fragrance. It is an essential spice in curry dishes.

Cinnamon Made from the dried bark of a tropical tree is available in small sticks or ground. It is deliciously fragrant and used to great effect in both savory and sweet dishes. The sticks are not edible and may be removed before serving, or used as a garnish or decoration.

Cloves These dried unopened flower buds should be used with care as they are rather pungent in flavor and can become overpowering if used in quantity. Whole cloves are decorative but not meant to be eaten and may be removed before serving.

Cumin Available as seeds or ground, cumin has a warm, pungent, aromatic flavor and is used extensively in Indian cooking.

Garam Masala is a ground aromatic mixture of spices that usually includes cardamom, cinnamon, cumin, cloves, peppercorns and nutmeg. It is used during and toward the end of cooking, or is sprinkled over dishes just before serving as an aromatic garnish. This spice mix is available ready-mixed, or you can make your own: finely grind together 1 tsp each black peppercorns and cumin seeds with 1 tbsp cardamom seeds, 8 whole cloves, a 2 in cinnamon stick or piece of cassia bark and about ¼ freshly grated nutmeg. Store in an airtight container and use within 3 weeks.

Ginger Fresh gingerroot looks like a knobbly stem and should be peeled before being chopped or grated before use. Fresh ginger has a refreshing, pungent flavor and is an essential ingredient in many Indian dishes. Also available ready minced in jars.

Nutmeg Available as whole nutmegs or grated – best to buy them whole and grate them yourself to fully appreciate the warm, sweet and aromatic flavor.

Paprika This bright-red powder comes from a variety of red pepper and is frequently used in cooking to add color to dishes. Although similar in color to cayenne pepper, paprika has a mild flavor and can be used in far greater quantity than cayenne.

Peppercorns are available in three colors – as white (ripe berries), black (unripened berries dried until dark green-black in colour) and green (unripe berries). It is the black peppercorns with their warm, aromatic flavor that are most frequently used in Indian cooking. The peppercorns are used whole (in dishes such as biryani, when they are not meant to be eaten and should be left on the side of the plate) or they may be ground, in which case they should be freshly milled as required for once ground they quickly lose flavor.

Saffron Comes from the stigmas of a species of crocus. It gives a distinctive flavor and rich, yellow coloring to dishes. Saffron is available in small packages or jars – powdered or in strands – the strands have a better flavor.

Turmeric is an aromatic root, closely related to ginger, which is dried and ground to produce a bright orange-yellow powder. It has a warm, distinctive smell and delicate, earthy flavor, and helps give dishes an attractive yellow coloring, but should not be used instead of saffron. Turmeric should be used with care as it can stain.

COOK'S SPICE NOTES

For the best flavor, buy the whole spices and grind them as and when required,

Tasty Accompaniments continued.

Carrot, raisin and onion salad
Coarsely grate 1⅓ cups carrots into a bowl. Peel and quarter 1 onion, cut into paper-thin slices and add to the carrots. Stir in 3 tbsp seedless raisins and 1 tbsp lemon juice. Season with ¼ tsp paprika, ½ tsp grated fresh gingerroot, salt and freshly ground black pepper. If wished, add slivers of fresh chili (or a little minced chili, from a jar) for a more fiery flavor. Mix all the ingredients together well and leave to stand for 30 minutes before serving, to allow time for the flavors to develop. Serve at room temperature or chilled.

DRINKS

When serving spicy dishes be sure to have a supply of refreshing drinks to hand – chilled mineral water, iced water or fruit juice are excellent choices. For special occasions and for a deliciously refreshing drink to sip during a hot, spicy meal, serve iced water flavored with spices, such as cardamom, cumin, cassia or cinnamon. Wine is not good served with Indian foods, because the taste is overpowered by the strong flavors of the food, so opt instead for chilled beers. You could also provide a jug of Lassi – a delicious and nutritious Indian drink of lightly spiced yogurt which is designed to cool the palate.

To MAKE LASSI: put 2½ cups plain yogurt in a blender or food processor with 6¼ cups cold water, 1-2 tsp lemon juice, 1 tbsp chopped fresh mint, ½ tsp each salt and dry-roasted cumin and freshly ground black pepper to taste. Blend for about 1 minute, then serve in a pitcher or tall glasses filled with crushed ice.

To MAKE SWEET LASSI: omit the lemon juice, mint, salt, cumin and pepper and instead flavor the yogurt and water with sugar, ground cardamom and a little rosewater, to taste. Blend as above and serve over crushed ice.

using a mortar and pestle or rolling pin, for small quantities, and a small electric coffee grinder for larger amounts. Whole spices keep their flavor and aroma far longer than ready-ground spices.

If you prefer to make the most of the ready-ground spices, buy them in small quantities and store them in a cool, dry, dark place in airtight jars and remember that once opened the spices begin to lose flavor and aroma. Roasting or dry-frying spices is a technique applied in Indian cooking which brings out a certain flavor and roasted aroma from spices and, at the same time makes them easier to crush. Use a heavy-based skillet and fry the whole spices in a dry pan (without oil or liquid) over a moderate heat, shaking the pan and stirring the spices until they turn a shade darker. (Take care not to overheat or the flavor of the spices becomes bitter). As soon as you smell the roasted aroma from spices, tip them onto a plate at once. Cool and use as required.

CUPBOARD STANDBYS

We are almost spoilt for choice with the excellent range of commercially prepared products now available in supermarkets. So, when time is at a premium, make the most of these "convenience" items. Spice mixes such as curry powders, garam masala and tandoori spices, plus the ready made curry pastes, sauces and jars of ready minced chili and fresh gingerroot are invaluable for making quick and authentic-tasting Indian dishes. There is also a wonderful selection of accompaniments available to include with your homemade dishes –

delicious items like poppadums, naan bread, chapatis, parathas, samosas and onion bhajis, plus a tempting range of Indian pickles and chutneys to choose from.

Cilantro (herb) Fresh cilantro is a favorite herb in Indian cooking. The green leaves (rather similar in appearance to flat-leaved parsley) are used extensively in dishes for flavoring and as a garnish. It is now widely available in supermarkets and specialist gourmet food stores, but if you have difficulty buying cilantro, use fresh flat-leaf parsley as a substitute.

Chilies Fresh chilies vary in hotness according to variety. Remember that the seeds are the hottest part, so it is up to you whether you include some or not. Always handle chilies with caution, preferably wearing rubber gloves because the juices are extremely pungent. Wash hands, utensils, board or work surface thoroughly after preparing and handling chilies and do not get your fingers near your eyes as this can be very painful. For convenience, make use of the ready-minced chili available in jars.

Ghee Indian cooks sometimes like to use ghee, for cooking. It gives a deliciously rich, nutty flavor to dishes and a glossy sheen to curried sauces and can be cooked at high temperatures without burning. However, vegetable oil may be used in any of the recipes here, in place of the ghee, if preferred. Ghee comes in two forms and can be bought from Asian grocers. It is worth noting that ghee, made from melted butter, is not suitable for vegans, although there is a vegetable ghee available from many Indian grocers and some health-food stores. To make your own ghee: melt unsalted butter in a saucepan and simmer gently for about 20 minutes until it becomes clear and a white residue settles at the bottom of the mixture. Remove the pot from the heat and skim off any scum from the surface. Leave the mixture to cool, then strain off the clear liquid and use as required. It will keep for up to 3 months stored in a container in the refrigerator.

Coconut Coconut is used extensively in Indian cooking to add flavor and creaminess to various dishes and sauces (both savory and sweet). The best flavor comes from freshly grated coconut, although ready-prepared shredded coconut makes an excellent standby.

Fresh grated coconut freezes successfully, so is well worth preparing when you've time to spare. Break the coconut in half, drain off the liquid and remove the flesh from its shell. Using a potato peeler, remove the brown skin, break the flesh into pieces and process in a food processor until finely grated. You can, if preferred, grate larger pieces on a cheese grater. Pack in small usable quantities and freeze for up to 3 months. Thaw and use as required.

Coconut products Coconut milk and creamed coconut are two popular ingredients in Indian cooking – the milk is available in cans, and creamed coconut comes in 7-8 oz packages at Indian grocery stores. To make your own coconut milk, chop a package of creamed coconut and place in a measuring jug. Add enough boiling water to come to the 2½ cups mark and stir to dissolve. Cool and use as required. Coconut cream is a thick, sweetened mixture that can be used in desserts.

Yogurt Yogurt plays an important part in vegetarian Indian cooking for it is used not only as a creamy flavoring in numerous dishes and sauces, but also as an accompaniment to hot dishes. If the yogurt is thick, stir or beat it for a few seconds to thin the consistency before using. Yogurt is frequently stirred into dishes toward the end of cooking and can become separated if overheated. To prevent this happening, blend the yogurt with a little cornstarch before heating – you require ½ tsp to every ⅔ cup yogurt – this helps stabilize the mixture and prevents it from separating when cooked. Alternatively, add the yogurt to the cooked mixture, a spoonful at a time, stirring well to incorporate it into the mixture before adding the next spoonful.

Rice Long-grain rice is the most widely available and the cheapest, although basmati rice with its slender grains and fine aromatic flavor is the best variety to use for Indian savory dishes whenever possible. Basmati rice is more expensive, so save it for special occasions if you cannot afford to use it every time.

There are many varieties of rice on the market, as well as numerous packages of quick-cook and precooked types, which makes it almost impossible to give exact cooking times, so if unsure, the best advice is to follow the package directions

ROASTED SPICE MIX

This is a very handy mixture to keep in your cupboard. The roasted, ground mixture can be kept in an airtight container. Add 1 teaspoonful when cooking rice, curries, dals or stews to give a quick and easy Indian flavor to your dishes.

4 tbsp cilantro seeds
1 tbsp cumin seeds

1. Heat a small skillet over a medium heat. When hot, add the seeds and toast over the heat until they turn a few shades darker.

2. Remove the pan from the heat and let the seeds cool slightly.

3. Place the seeds in a coffee grinder and grind as finely as possible. Alternatively, grind the seeds in a mortar and pestle. Store in an airtight container.

DAL

Dal are actually split peas, lentils and beans. There are several different kinds available, which can all be used to make the dal that you will find on the menu in Indian restaurants.

1 ¹/₃ cups chana dal or yellow
    split peas, soaked
5 cups water
¹/₂ tsp turmeric
1 onion, chopped
1 tsp ground cumin
2 tbsp vegetable oil
¹/₂ tsp mustard seeds
2 garlic cloves, crushed
2 dried chilies, seeded and
    chopped
1 ¹/₂ cups canned chopped
    tomatoes
salt and pepper

1. Drain and rinse the lentils then place in a saucepan with the water and turmeric. Bring to a boil then cover and simmer for 30 minutes.

2. Add the onion and cumin, stir, cover and cook for another 15 minutes.

3. Meanwhile, heat the oil in a small saucepan and add the mustard seeds. When the seeds pop, add the chilies and tomatoes. Cook for 2-3 minutes, then add the contents of the pan to the lentils. Stir well, add salt and pepper to taste and serve.

to ensure good results. Rice (especially basmati) should be rinsed in a strainer under cold running water before cooking to rid it of the starchy residue left from the milling process. Brown rice is the whole unpolished grain with only the tough outer hull removed. It has a nutty flavor and chewy texture and therefore contains larger amounts of vitamins, minerals and protein than the white polished rice. It takes longer to cook than white rice, generally about 40 minutes. It may be used in any recipes which call for long-grain rice, but if the dish is cooked by the absorption method (such as a biryani), you will need to allow extra liquid and a longer cooking time.

Legumes (dal) Dried beans, peas and lentils are an essential ingredient in the vegetarian diet, helping provide a large portion of the daily protein requirement – and Indian cooking is renowned for its interesting and delicious range of legume dishes. However, although these legumes (known collectively as dal) are rich in protein, they are not a complete protein in themselves and need to be served with either a grain (such as rice) and/or a bread (naan, chapatis, pooris or parathas), plus a dairy product like yogurt or cheese.

Legumes come in a range of colours and shapes (round, oval, kidney-shaped or capsule like). They may be large, medium or small, whole or split (the splitting helps them cook much faster) and are sometimes skinned. There is a wide range of legumes available from supermarkets, health-food stores and Asian stores. It is important to check

legumes before cooking as the packets may contain small stones and husks which should be removed before using.

Whole dried legumes (with the exception of lentils) should be soaked overnight in cold water before cooking, or prepared by the quick-soak method: place the legume in a saucepan, cover with cold water and bring to a boil, then boil rapidly for 10 minutes. Remove the pan from the heat, cover and leave the beans to soak in the water for 3 hours. Once legumes have been soaked (by the slow or quick method), they should be drained, placed in a saucepan with fresh cold water to cover and boiled rapidly for 10 minutes to destroy the toxins present in some beans. The heat is then reduced and the legumes simmered for the required time given in a recipe. Cooking times vary according to the type of legume and its freshness.

Dried legumes keep for up to 6 months, after which time the skins begin to toughen, so it's best to buy them from a supermarket with a quick turnover to ensure you are getting fresh stock. Store the legumes in an airtight container. When seasoning legumes, add salt toward the end of cooking, never at the beginning because this tends to toughen the skins. For extra flavor add 1 or 2 garlic cloves or bay leaves, or an onion studded with cloves to the pot when boiling the legumes.

Here is a list of the more widely used legumes– all available from supermarkets.

Split red lentils Bright, shiny orange-red lentils with a pleasant, mild flavor. This type does not require soaking before cooking, and once cooked, breaks down to become soft and pulpy in texture. Used in many dishes, including soups, curries and sauces to thicken them and to add protein.

Lentils Green-brown lentils are larger and have a stronger flavor than the split red type. They retain their shape after cooking, although may be cooked for longer and mashed to a pulpy texture, if wished. This type is sometimes soaked for a time before cooking, or according to recipe directions and are used in all type of dishes such as vegetable koftas, soups, curried vegetable dishes and biryanis.

Chana dal Although similar in appearance to yellow split peas, chana dal is a hulled, split, black chick-pea, popular with vegetarians because of its high-protein content. It is not as widely available as other dals, although you will find it in some of the larger supermarkets, as well as at Indian grocery stores and some health-food stores. The recipes in this book use yellow split peas instead of chana dal, but the latter may be used instead, if wished.

Chick-peas These large, beige-colored peas are shaped like hazelnuts, and once cooked have a nutty flavor and slightly crunchy texture. Chick-peas are also ground to make gram (or besan flour) – a fine yellow flour that is used in a variety of dishes, including pakoras and onion bhajis. Chick-peas are also available ready cooked in cans.

Black-eye peas these oval-shaped peas are grayish or beige in colour with a dark dot in the center. They have a slightly smoky flavor and are excellent cooked in many dishes. Canned, ready cooked black-eye peas are also available.

Red kidney beans These large, deep red, kidney-shaped beans have a slightly nutty flavor and are excellent cooked in spicy sauces, soups and all types of vegetable dishes. Also available ready-cooked in cans.

Canned legumes Canned black-eye peas, red kidney beans and chick-peas are a convenient and quick alternative to the dried variety and are widely available in supermarkets. These legumes are cooked and ready to eat, but before using, empty them into a strainer to drain and rinse under cold running water before using as required. You will see that the recipes in this book use only the canned peas and chick-peas in order to cut out the lengthy cooking times otherwise involved, but the dried types may be used instead, if preferred, and the method of cooking and the cooking times adjusted accordingly. As the canned beans and peas tend to be quite soft in texture, they are more usually added to the various dishes toward the end of cooking time to prevent them from becoming over mushy.

BASMATI RICE

This is a foolproof way of cooking rice by the absorption method. Do not be tempted to lift the lid before the time is up, or the steam will escape and the rice will not be cooked.

1¼ cups basmati rice

1. Rinse the rice in several changes of water and drain thoroughly.

2. Place the rice in a heavy-based saucepan and add enough water so that the water level is 1 in above the surface of the rice.

3. Bring the rice to a vigorous boil, then stir well. Cover the pot tightly and turn off the heat. Leave the pan on the stove-top for 25 minutes, then lift off the stove and leave, still covered, for another 10 minutes. Fork up the rice and serve.

INDEX